Never Such Innocence Again

(Poems from War)

By

Jim McGarrah

ISBN: 978-93-6354-382-9

First Edition: 2025
Rs. 200/-

Cyberwit.net
HIG 45 Kaushambi Kunj, Kalindipuram
Allahabad - 211011 (U.P.) India
http://www.cyberwit.net
Tel: +(91) 9415091004
E-mail: info@cyberwit.net

Printed at Repro India Limited.

Acknowledgements

Of the fifteen books of mine that literary presses have published, this is the eighth collection of poems. All but a few newer poems were chosen from the earlier seven works randomly and collected in this volume because they dealt with the experience of war and the aftermath in some way. Thanks to these book publishers and all the magazines—some now defunct—that published these pieces over the past twenty-five years.

1. *Running the Voodoo Down (Elixir Press, 2007)*

2. *When the Stars Go Dark (Main Street Rag, 2009)*

3. *Breakfast at Denny's (Ink Brush Press, 2013)*

4. *The Truth About Mangoes (Lamar University Press, 2016)*

5. *A Balancing Act (Lamar University Press, 2018)*

6. *You Can Never Go Back to the Turtleback Inn (Rochak Publishing 2022)*

7. *News of the World and Other Places (Rochak Publishing, 2023)*

This book is dedicated to David Kelly,
more than my friend for over fifty years,
a brother-in-arms during the Tet Offensive
and through the struggle for peace ever since.

Omega

The dead
no longer need a self
to find peace.

There is no purpose
in a small disturbance
after the storm ends.

Author's Forward:

1. Coming Home Early Days:

Fear: He knew that he needed to be held. Part of his mind ordered him to bring someone close, stroke her hair, feel her heart and his beat together. Part of his mind recoiled with the fear of being touched, and this was the strongest, loudest, angriest, most hopeless part. The closer you bring someone to you, the farther you push them away. He had nothing to say. The physical power of words had been lost. Larger voices called, the hum of the fan in their bedroom, starlings whistling outside the window, a hungry cat squalling from the alley, the dead lying in dark back rooms and streets wiped clean of carnal attachments. Reality was only a lace curtain seen through when you weren't even looking, easily ripped apart and separated by time and space, connected by the thinnest of threads, but mostly a veil. He knew words existed, but his language was now different from the rest of the world. It rained before dawn, and he tried to count the drops as they—one two three—as they exploded against the windowpane into infinity. He had accepted death to survive. He was no stranger to irony—the hospital built next to a ski lodge, the biggest bass he ever saw broke water and snapped his line, his ex-wife married their divorce lawyer, his best friend's only sins were venial, the man confessed once a week, prayed constantly, and killed no one in his hometown. He did not believe in any god until that day when his squad gathered at the edge of the dense and dark jungle where the rice paddies ended. The mortar shell fell through the gloaming and after it fell, left only the silence of his friend in a perfume of jasmine, cordite, and blood. Then, he believed. He knew that God was death, the Terror of living.

Therapy: Framed by degrees books computers and a broken clock, his doctor sits amid this refuse of her clinical kingdom explaining the bond between the squeeze of a trigger and the rush of blood through the brain, the pain with joy as if you swallowed a whole bowl of ice cream all at once. "That is one inconsistency of war to men of good conscience." But she did not understand. No one knows, even an artist, what the primal mind chooses for its art—foreground, background, contrast, form, and substance—There is no search for sense in his thought anymore. Memories that bleed the brightest colors seek him out.

Blending In: In his favorite diner in his hometown in the early morning after coming home, he drinks his bitter coffee. The man at the counter on his right reads the news with feigned interest as if the print might be a bite of unbuttered toast. An old couple chew their scrambled eggs slowly like cows waiting for a truck to the abattoir. A young man in a white tee-shirt speaks with animated gestures to a forlorn waitress. Three grandmothers stuff their grandkids with pancakes and syrup. Outside the large window the sky folds over the highway as traffic comes and goes. The ebb and flow of ordinary life goes on while somewhere in his mind a bullet rips into flesh, a child lays across the unmoving corpse of his mother, jets whine low in the sunrise and the jungle explodes in fire. The scent of bacon and the clank of spoons against ceramic cups surrounds the room with a routine of life that has no knowledge of random death. Montaigne discovered four hundred years ago that nothing makes us remember it so well as the desire to forget it.

Re-Education: It begins by counting ceiling tiles during a lecture on fossils. Semoria is a reptilomorph named for a town in Texas. Winged lizards nested on the ground, unlike bats. Straight-ankle thedodants evolved into crocodiles and then, humans. He is learning these facts because his therapist told him education is the key to becoming a civilized human. In fact, he had known a thecodant in DaNang with perfect ankles. Her neck smelled like jasmine and vanilla and sweat. He paid her a dollar extra so she would whisper the name of his high school sweetheart as he came. He chose "Karen." "Anapsids, synapsis, diapsids all may have been warm-blooded," the professor's voice echoes along the classroom walls and his disconnected shadow flutters along with it under the blanched flicker of the overhead lights. The young woman in the seat next to him is warm blooded, and she is no fossil. She smells like honeysuckle; her hair is a blonde curtain that must be gently parted with his fingers to reach her thoughts. Her sighs of boredom distract him. They sound like spring rain kissing a small lake. "Vocalization among dinosaurs would strongly suggest social interaction," The professor chants his monotone mantra beside the blackboard. 'Some cataclysmic event ended their reign over the earth. All that we have left are fragments of their bones." What if dinosaurs died during TET in 1968, littering the city of Hue with their bones as the streets filled with smoke. He sits quietly among other students, learning that some knowledge is best kept to himself and so, pretends to be an actor in a great play who has been inspired not as much by character or plot, as the numb vacancy in his mind and a talent for being what he is not.

Dawn: Sunrise began to sneak through the breezy cracks in the old farmhouse as the amphetamines wore through his brain. Sunlight and shadows hopscotched across the furniture and floor. Hours must have passed in the cloud of smoke from burning cigarettes. His voice sounded like wet sandpaper on metal. No one had moved away from the group of friends gathered for his confession. A woman held him, and the rest of them sat at his feet. He began to feel empty. The oil of his being poured out on the heads of disciples, anointing them with his knowledge of philosophical treatises, theological mythology, sociological ramifications, and feral theories on the fall of man in war. He stood and took the woman by the hand and spoke no more. They climbed the stairs in the old farmhouse. They made love and slept. When he woke up, it was twilight of the same day. Cold and alone, even with a warm body beside him, the idea that he might be dying crowded into his thoughts. Opening the only window in the room, he crawled out on the roof as the sun folded itself into the earth. Blackness began to creep forward from the horizon, covering the gray so slowly he could feel the planet rotating on its axis. The spring warmth came apart like wet newspaper and the air chilled. The smell of dead flowers overwhelmed him, and he didn't know where it came from. The lilacs and tulips had yet to even bloom. He sat wondering if they ever would.

2. Certifiable

My being a veteran injured in war
gets my widow two thousand dollars
toward funeral expenses provided
she can prove that I died of a disease
causally related to said war and if she
presents bureaus within bigger bureaus
notarized forms that verify my passing.
I have official letters from Congress
that specify this fact. Otherwise,
she gets two hundred and fifty dollars
for a death recorded as unsuitably fatal.

“A true war story is never moral. It does not instruct, nor encourage virtue, nor suggest models of proper human behavior, nor restrain men from doing the things men have always done. If a story seems moral, do not believe it. If at the end of a war story you feel uplifted, or if you feel that some small bit of rectitude has been salvaged from the larger waste, then you have been made the victim of a very old and terrible lie. There is no rectitude whatsoever. There is no virtue. As a first rule of thumb, therefore, you can tell a true war story by its absolute and uncompromising allegiance to obscenity and evil.” – Tim O Brien, from *The Things They Carry*

Example:

All these years from the TET Offensive
a car crashes and the Life Flight helicopter swoops so low
over the tree line, its black shadow clips the back of my head.
Those turbines whine and rotors slap air with a rhythmic thud,
then Jim Morrison chants, “this is the end, beautiful end my friend...”,
then my left knee aches for whiskey to dull the pain,
then I’m forced to drink beer warm, and eat powdered eggs cold,
then rain pours for days and those days fall down like rain,
then I can’t sleep someone pops the tab on a Pepsi can,
slides a deadbolt home in the dark, bumps my bad leg, or steps behind me;
then summer sours the river, cypress molds and I smell fish rotting,
then the wind screams, the sky explodes, bone sears into red powder,
air fills my lungs like bits of broken glass, and those already dead
continue dying, charred slivers of wood and stone. Hell, years
later I’m still hiding, nauseous and naked, in the napalmed jungle.

(from *Running the Voodoo Down*)

Contents

Soldier's Heart

That's what Army surgeons called it
when Blue fought Gray, as if shooting your brother
was a romantic notion cloying, like honeysuckle,
in the ante bellum air. When the mortars
and gas filled the trenches of Europe
with sleepless nights and body parts, you were
shell-shocked, as if your mind were electric,
short-circuited by the surge of death around you.
Today, numbness has become
pragmatic and politically correct.
The new term is Post Traumatic Stress
Disorder, as if the mind were a deck of cards
stacked on the kitchen table waiting to be swatted
by a child's hand on the way to the cookie jar,
as if Freddie Johnson hadn't caught a bouncing betty
waist high like a handoff in a high school
football game, as if Billy Wolfe hadn't cut a penis
from an NVA soldier's body and stuffed it like an apple
in the dead mouth, as if Rick Santos hadn't eaten
his own bullet and left the back of his head all over
your new handmade in Hong Kong silk shirt, as if
limbless children and their faceless mothers
don't recoil through your brain every time some
asshole at a party yells *incoming* to see if you'll twitch.
Yeah, yeah…'Nam's been over fifty years, so quit
whining. There are new wars being fought, new labels
placed on old pain, new methods to fog memory.
Quit bitching. You're alive. That's more than you can say
for Phuc Tran and Phil Jansen, caught on opposite ends

of the same ambush the night you got your first clean kill.
life goes on…suck it up…get real…it's in the past…
you know the clichés. You've got them memorized by now
and chant them like the mantra of that one Buddhist bonze
squatting in the marketplace at Gia Le, doused
with gasoline and trying to strike a match in the monsoon breeze.

Guernica

(on seeing Picasso's famous painting)

What I don't remember is what I should,
that one day in April when a child plays
next to her mother's leg in the marketplace
of a small Basque town called Guernica.
She smells lilacs and mountain vetch,
newly tanned leather, coriander and cloves,
the hint of wine on the sausage vendor's breath.
All around her a warm breeze makes the pine trees
laugh, as the reds and blues of spring
buzz through the street in the shape of other children.
She has no idea what it means to be alive,
but feels a wild current surge through her arms and legs
as if she were the lightning rod on the schoolhouse roof
two hundred meters up the cobbled street.

When the Luftwaffe burns through the bright sky,
their engines humming softly, this girl has
no knowledge of her death. Giant Steel Birds
migrate to nest in her village. When they swoop
to tree top height, she waves. The pilots smile back
and then open the bomb bay doors to drop their gift
of random death. This is no brutal illusion art creates,
no future statement against the terror of war.
So, I force myself to think of painting, like Picasso
who sat alone in his studio, and I wonder why
he chose the absence of bright reds on his canvas,
the angular gray faces on broken bodies rising in silence,
the dead greens and grays for background, like fog rising
in the summer rain, offering water back to the useless sun.

Portrait in Shades of Blues

My father would have changed places
if he could have. I don't mean white
to black or with a desire to suffer
needlessly. He was no martyr, a hero
from WWII maybe, but he denied
that label as well. What drove him
was more complex than revising race
or moving to a ghetto, simpler than
switching color. He gambled, cursed,
attended church, gave money to charities,
did business with everyone in the county
as an honest and helpful man who made
no enemies that didn't deserve to be.
A white man in the Eisenhower era,
he watched Fred Astaire movies
at the theater and played Bing Crosby
on a jukebox at our small-town VFW.
My father showed his family love as he
was taught love should be shown,
with grace, patience, and duty.
But when his world became a sad place
full of memories, he bought cheap whiskey,
and retreated to a small room in our large home
with a stack of records, a paper cup, and a bag
full of ice. There he sat with his true friends,
numbed by the war he had fought and a life
he never asked for. I remember him wailing
along with each record, the sound leeching
through a crack in the French doors,

along the hallway, and into my bedroom
late at night as his offkey voice shared
in the melody everything wrong and everything
right with the world, even though my father
could never carry a tune further than his mind.
His choir had magical names—Blind Willie,
John Lee Hooker, Skip James, Son House,
Ray Charles, Robert Johnson, Furry Lewis
and Pinetop Perkins. They sang strange words
about crossroads and killing floors and the joyful
dangers of love with a feeling that my father knew
war had taken and with the voice he wanted back.

Parker's Crossing, Tennessee – October 31, 2011

The store is a "middle-of-nowhere" place
stuffed with Confederate flags, toy muskets,
cheap statues of Nathan Bedford Forrest,
and peanut brittle. I've stopped for fuel
at Parker's Crossing because the tank's empty
and to quote my old man on his gambling days –
"This is the only game in town."

My ghosts have always been silent
even on Halloween, but over the pump and flow
of fuel, beneath the cries of flocking crows,
beyond the clicking gallon counter,
and despite my wife's happy chatter,
sounds no longer from this natural world
rise in empty fields behind the building.

If I'm lucky, I'm insane and the sound
carried on the autumn air is not real.
This explains with less terrifying logic
the human moans from a thick-throated wind,
the drum of boots on scarred earth, rifle fire,
the thud of northern steel against the soft flesh
of southern pride and the rush of a current

in the blood-red creek bed dry for a hundred years.
It's all so vivid, as if wind bridged echoes
of brother crying over dying brother with a boy

burned by fire in my own, more recent, war dreams,
as if this simple store was built on blanched bones
and filled with cheap souvenirs to hide one fact.
The only monuments worthy of war are ghosts.

Chagall's "The Poet Reclining"

(Painted During WWI in 1915)

The barn is fenced by fir trees, one pig in the sty
and a dappled horse tethered and grazing nearby.

In the foreground of the canvas a man lies with his head
on a folded beige jacket, hands clasped across his chest
in funereal pose, a crumpled hat tossed behind him casually.

From the expressionless face narrow slits replace eyes
that might be closed or merely squinting in an impotent attempt

to not notice what, as a poet, he must discern estranged
from any artist's pastoral ideal—a war being fought
around the edges of Chagall's canvas. His calm demeanor

is betrayed by the ashen pallor on his face and beyond
the horizon's vanishing point, a ravaged violet sky.

Nachthexen, or the Night Witches of Russia

Darkness formed their only shield
against the ack-ack. Forty bi-planes,
tiny and made from wood
and canvas flew thirty thousand
bombing runs into the Nazi heart.
The planes were so old and tired
that men refused to fly them.
But these pilots painted wings
with flowers and from their flying
wombs gave birth to bombs.
They glossed their lips
with plotting pencils to remind
the men that courage
was a female trait and war,
the lethal brother of them all.
Stalin praised the brave sisters
of the motherland, and then purged
their families from the soil the pilots
died to protect for his fear that females
might be worshipped more than him.

The Shit Wars in 1966

My last spring in high school
pigeons attacked the clock tower
atop the county courthouse.
Hundreds roosted in cracks and crevices
along the gutters and on the roof.
Pigeon shit painted the town square.
The flying grey rats shat on lawyers,
the old circuit judge, the county clerk
and the beehive hairdos of her all-female
staff, even the credit criminals
as they snuck into a court for bad debts.
These winged demons held no regard
for status or beauty. They dive-bombed
Cadillac's and Chevy's alike. They defaced
park benches and Civil War statues.

Enough was enough. The mayor phoned
our county game warden who arrived
one morning with a dozen shotguns
loaded with double ought buck shot
and a coffee thermos full of bourbon.
I skipped class to watch the carnage
through the plate-glass window
of the Palace Pool Hall across the street.

For three hours it rained feathers and blood.
The sky filled with blue smoke. The air stank
of cordite and bird entrails as gunfire rattled
shop windows and the merchants carped

like scalded dogs. Pigeon parts were carted
off the sidewalks by a gang of feral cats.
My friends seemed filled with bloodlust
and cheered as the body count rose.
I was ambivalent regarding bird murder
but did not want to be embarrassed
by a less than manly attitude and so,
I enlisted in the Marine Corps that summer.

Herkimer, New York

(in memory of James Bagby)

It's just off an interstate ramp,
an oasis of low budget motels,
a row of half-empty taverns
with soot-covered windows
and bug-splattered, burned out
neon signs. A few closed stores
and small diner full of hunger
dot the main street. I stop here
for lunch, one of those places
my father would have described
as "the only game in town"
on any given Sunday.

The waitress brings a plate
full of roast beef that stares at me
with the same over-cooked angst
as the waitress. Outside the window,
a murder of crows pecks at rocks
and hop over a rainbow of oil stains
in the puddled parking lot.
This place is an Edward Hopper
painting on barbiturates.

I'm driving through on my way
to somewhere else, and I remember
my friend Jim who died last week
alone and surrounded by thousands

of people in downtown Houston.
This was the way he lived his life,
always going through somewhere
on the way to someplace else.

He wanted to write books,
even if no one reads them,
as a way to say
what he could never say out loud.
So, he bought himself
a used typewriter for ten bucks.

I'm drinking coffee and re-reading
the only thing Jim ever typed.
It came in the mail two days ago,
mailed by a stranger after Jim's death
hidden by four motel walls and a curtain
of rage that could keep him alive no longer.

I keep returning to the first sentence
that he typed as a fitting epitaph
for all of us who wandered through
decades of dark memories of a war
no one really wanted and that we fought
out of curiosity, need, embarrassment,
or because our number came up.
The death we carried inside our lives
left us outside our lives.

"This thing keeps running off the page.
Maybe I'll learn to set the margins later"

Visiting the Museum of Hostages, Slovenia, 2003

(*"Cowards die many times before their deaths.*
The valiant never taste of death but once.")
—William Shakespeare

In this photograph a young man stands,
awaiting death like it's the next bus home.
He's bound to a bullet-scarred tree,
his eyes half-closed as if he rests
after having fed on ripe strawberries
from a picnic lunch, as if the blue flame
of sky and a bottle of good Riesling
made him drowsy and content, unaware
of the Nazi pill boxes and trenches I see
that still ring the field with memories of hate.

The guide explains that these silent cell blocks
once locked away a whole town of farmers
and their families. One morning, they were
set free to flee the Russians marching
through the Soca Valley like red ants
devouring all human flesh in their path,
or so the Nazi soldiers told them.

The prisoners ran, blinded by their lust
for liberty more than fear of its reason.

When the fir trees along the hillcrest spread
out before them like pillars from heaven,

machine guns inside the bunkers spat
unrestrained fire. Weeping women fell
like stones and covered children. The men
turned and fought the lead wind with bare hands.
Blood and flesh roiled like wheat chaff in the field.

I asked why this man was tied and shot last.
"He refused to leave his cell, therefore his captors
made him watch his family die first."

The Moon Walk, July 20, 1969

Drunk, I follow the tracks behind the Legion Hall,
and scoop cinders honeycombed from the heat
of locomotives chugging freight through town,
toss them at glass insulators atop the telephone poles
that line the tracks, hoping I might hit one finally
as the holey stones whistle through the vapid air.

My wish carried home from Vietnam—to be
a child again, re-live Sandy Koufax dreams
out here on Hall's Hill, and crossing the tracks, pierce
the thick woods of oaks, elderberries, pines behind
the hardware store, snake through my secret briar patch
and flower onto a meadow full of dandelions, to go back

while the world goes forward and cheers strange men
in white suits who, unlike the fallen in every war,
will come alive again from the womb of a black sky.

Masters of War

1. North

Across the road, two horses buck and run, playing tag,
and stopping to snack on the fescue that floors
the field in which they live. I call them Red and Blackie
for the benefit of Dog, who I named as well.

The dog can't see colors. She understands neither those names
nor the word respect but believes we all deserve respect
as neighbors who will only be neighbors once in this lifetime.
Are we masters of the world by virtue of the power in language?

The horses remind me of a photo I saw a black and white
Daguerreotype of General William Tecumseh Sherman astride
a bay stallion, both man and beast next to a field cannon.
The caption below the photo reads: *I am sick and tired of war.*

The words are owned by Sherman,
but the horse would speak them if it could see the gray
in colors—the sky blue and cloudless, trees in verdant green,
the field full of flowering clover covered by rich red dew.

2. South

At Oakland Park Cemetery in Atlanta
On a Sunday morning in June
Magnolias bloom a bitter white
flowered by silent sunlight.

Around their frail arrogance
purple hydrangeas bow in submission.
There is no breeze as I stand on ground
General John B. Hood held as he watched
while Sherman burned his beloved city

The scent of lavender
hovers above rows of blanched gravestones
like the sickly sweetness of cotton candy
after the carnival has left the midway.
The stones stand at attention, an army
of cold marble behind Hood's cenotaph
that leads them in battle to meet the last enemy.
But here there is no sound of trumpets
no King and angels to conquer Death
only brittle bones and flesh gone to seed
in the red Georgia clay.

It was said the light of battle shone in Hood's eyes,
that he believed in cause, cross, and crown.
But I choose to think the brightness more
a sign from flames reflected on his Quixote face,
a keen awakening that one day all the marrow
of his warriors would mingle with the dust
of his slaves buried in the plots next to theirs
as Hood's tall and thin shadow remains over them all.

3. Gods

In the Beginning
when humanity was a small thing,
like a rash on the wrist of earth, we built

our gods from clay, calling the first one Ishtar.
We gave her power over Love
bowing down before we grasped the power
of Love compelled her to make War as well.

Alter Idem

(poetry reading in the Balkans, 2001)

We stood
one at a time
in various stages
of composition,
chanting
wild vowels
and consonants
as if the same
wool blanket woven
from different
languages might warm
us all, as if
smoke rising
in the room
might mingle
somewhere over
our heads,
signal us into the past
and remind us
that a few paved miles
ringed by mountains
were once all we had
between us,
not the ocean
of rhetoric
or the demagogues
that waged the wars,

or leftover landmines
that rip the legs and arms
from future generations
who may never
understand:
the first walls that must
come down
are ones bricked
with words.

Rearview Mirror in Italy

The woman at the café table across from mine scrubs
purple jelly from her boy's face. A blush rises
in its place and stains his skin. Monet saw daybreak
as the time without time when he painted
Impression: Sunrise, skimming and dipping
the brush through morning fog, fixing movement
of light between sun and small skiff, touching
the silence of substance in the heart of form. Me?
I can't paint, not this morning or any other. Still,
when the boy's tears begin, days arc from my mind,
flow over the fan-shaped, cobbled square, and fade
into the brown canvas of Sienna, Italy.

I'm spending my life borrowing time from corpses.

"A picaresque hero," my friend Leslie says, "a myth
that lives as if his own breath is a not a mystery."

Leslie's wrong. In this place, that myth comes undone
when the boy lays his crying head on his mother's arm
reminding me that all myths are always more than real.

My own is taller, more handsome, braver,
and the language it speaks is less scarred. Years ago
it saved Bobby Wolfe from stepping on a land mine,
and pulled Rick's rifle barrel away from his own chin
before he jerked the trigger and blew his brains across
the front of my new shirt. My myth never slit a throat
for refusing *chu hoi* one night on a dark jungle trail.

The myth of me has appetites that know no limits,
never feels alone in rooms full of people, and never asks
why his friend dies, and he lives through the bomb blast
every day for ten thousand nine hundred and fifty days.
It's legendary in liaisons with women and forgetful
of its own failed marriages. The myth prophecies,
walking into the wilderness barefoot and bone-tired
in search of mystic stones. It's an angel who brings
a message to deaf generations, a dragon that breathes
the unquenchable fire of life into a god's mouth, a lover
who dances naked into the wild Tuscan night and ends up
quietly watching a boy and his mother share grape jelly.

Ghost Pain

An old barstool stands
in the kitchen between stove
and counter. My father used to sit
there before dawn, read the Racing Form
in the yellow light of a bare bulb,
drink coffee, eat Bran flakes,
and wait for my mother to scream
that whole last year before she died.
No one sits there anymore.
Four steel legs stain the floor
as if the tile were infected with rust.
I walk past each day feeling the way
John Gibson must have felt
after his leg was blown
off by a B-40 rocket round
in the '68 Tet Offensive. He lay
in the hospital bed next to mine and clawed
the empty sheet, begging for morphine.
The nurse always laughed.
"That's just *ghost pain*," she'd say
and boot him up with another 5 cc's.

Tune-Up

The man who fixes my car
came from Jordan,
doesn't drink booze,
fasts during Ramadan, and
never built a bomb.

The only terrorists he knows are his small children
who behave much the same as mine did at an early age
and a wife that makes him scrub grease from under
his nails before daring to sit down to dinner.

He treats me fairly,
does good work,
has never overcharged
anyone I know
for his labor.

I would not kill this man for any god and do not fear
for my life when the oil gets changed in my Ford. I call
him friend and might even loan him money, if I had some.
He would not send a drone to my daughter's wedding.

"War, what is it good for? Absolutely nothing.
Say it again…War…" - Edwin Hawkins

When a Zero Means Everything

Three hundred and eleven, 311, three eleven.
Like all numbers, it's useful no matter how it's written.
It can describe the number of chews you took
to swallow a piece of gristle on an overcooked roast,
define the steps from your bed to the bathroom
as your prostrate ages, list the number of free cable
channels on the TV in your cheap motel room.
Three hundred and eleven may be the days after
your birthday or the days before Christmas.
Apart or together the digits mean nothing specific
and anything possibly depending on context.
They hold no guilt, anger, fear, or honor no matter
whispered or shouted, printed or scrawled.
But do this. Circle a zero in front of three
—0311—
at your Marine Corps recruitment office.
Then, the numbers are steps through a minefield,
rounds before the rifle jams, shadows at dusk,
seconds before air support, nights without sleep,
ways to lose a life, ways to take a life,
or a simple cue of how mankind can't quite
quantify its own value without dying.

Eating with Chopsticks in Vietnam

"L'homme est ne' libre." – Rousseau
 "L'homme est ne' poltron" – Conrad

Eating with chopsticks was an art not easily mastered,
or so I learned when the village elders led my squad
beneath the tiled roof of the old French schoolhouse
and fed us *cahn cho* in wooden bowls.
I choked it down with red rice wine in the heat
of the Lunar New Year and mastered the art
before the meal ended. Laughing, I balanced one grain
between those two sticks of wood while the air filled
with sweat and ginger, while the sniper steadied
his rifle in the twist of a banyan tree.
Marty pointed at my success and babbled like a child
who had just noticed the wonder in a rose petal
before he dropped face first into the scalding duck soup,
as if the sniper's bullet had pried open a small door
above his eyes, crawled in, and flicked the switch off.
In that split second, I could have painted substance
inside a shadow, written a book that breathed, sculpted
a living form from marble or composed a score in silence.
I was a prophet, a Jeremiah in jungle boots who saw
the world's future between the rice stuck on the wood
and the blood and bone stuck on my face like wet sand.
Then, I ran for cover and hid behind a chipped stone wall.

Learning Curve

1.

The Battle of Passchendaele, 1917
In the rain and blood
the mud rusted red
as back and forth
inches at a time
armies went.
It was claimed to be
too late "a senseless campaign."
Half-a-million men lost
and nothing gained.
The crows cried for days.
It was impossible to know
if they cried in joy or sorrow.

2.

The Battle of Hue, 1968
He's fourteen years old and already dead,
splayed on barb wire like a squirrel on a spit.
His mother leaves the burning joss stick inside
a roadside altar close by as she carries a basket
full of balut—those fermented duck babies
women eat in the shells to strengthen a fetus
of their own in the womb.

Time is too short for incidental grief in war.
You are young compared to her, but old to death.
The smell of rotted flesh and moldy earth

no longer make you cringe as you rise
from the bunker, piss in a trough,
brush your teeth with brackish water, and listen
to her screams as if she were a peacock mating.

You load your rifle as the salmon-colored sun melts
across banyan trees, as ghosts shimmer from the hot mist
that floats above the rice paddies, as all thought dissolves
into the primal ooze of your survival. The woman wails
in a language you don't understand or care to learn.
What you came to say has been spoken and what
she answers will take you years of pain to translate.

Nuance in 'Nam

The more I saw of war, the more
I notice the difference
between words like fucking
and making love.

It took me years to understand
how words can remake memories.

War becomes
the melody of toucans
composing in banyan trees.
Pain lives in the warm sunrise
as it gives birth to lotus flowers
from the wombs of jungle waters.
Death rides a soft breeze before the storm.

Einstein's Theory Is Relative

When I was wounded in a firefight
my friend Tri, standing next to me,
caught a bullet in his chest.
We laid in a ditch for fourteen minutes
while he coughed and died.

Hours seemed to pass.

The first day after my war was over
I lay beside a beautiful woman,
both of us naked and high on cocaine.
We laughed from midnight till dawn.

Minutes seemed pass.

Now, I'm old. Time is a construct
that I want to run away from.

Days pass in seconds.

Daybreak on the Morning of Tet, 1968

A man sits in the door
of a Huey helicopter
that brushes the top
of a lowland rain forest
in northern Quang Tri
—fig trees, banyans,
bamboo, douc langur
rest on their limbs.
Beneath the broad shade
coffee farms, spiders & snails,
a white tiger with her cubs
all rest in silence
and the calm fragrance
of woodsmoke rises
from a pho fire.
Children are eating breakfast.

The copter blades whir
in sync with his racing
heartbeat, a rapid metallic
thump…thump…thump

The cloudless sky
fills with the songs
from the jungle—a cry
from a harpy eagle,
fish splash in a river,
the white tiger roars,
a breeze echoes through

a meadow full of orchids.
The man with twelve others,
clears the copter blades,
& wades into what
he has just flown above.
Nothing in the morning
changes as everything does.

The Memorial Wall in Washington, D.C.

"Of what benefit to me is the multitude of your sacrifices?" says Jehovah. "I have had enough of whole burnt offerings and the fat of well-fed animals; and in the blood of young bulls." and male lambs and he goats I have taken no delight." - Isaiah 1:11

1 - Arrival

You said Quang Tri was quiet when compared to Detroit
on Saturday night. I, being corn fed, believed you.
"Quiet as an old whore's bedroom," you said,
until the first whistle exploded and spilled
a mouthful of Tiger beer down my chin,
spraying the bolt on my new M-16. You grinned.

That smirk calmed all my fears
born in a place where ten seconds was a lifetime.
We lunged into a bunker when the next shell hit,
puppy clumsy. Like kids playing football,
chasing a fumble, we laughed, tumbling into darkness.

2 - Halfway Home

Rice wine burned us both, but opium seared
the marrow from your boyish conscience.
Disappointed, you asked why I'd fired too far left.
The kid was pulling up his pants, an easy target
in twilight. He reminded me of a robin I'd shot
with my BB gun, squatting, pecking the wet ground

unaware of my existence, or its own thin mortality.
I was ten then and crying.

Your smile froze after six months in that country,
hiding a heart hardened by a dozen firefights
and memories sewn into body bags.
Those eyes, glistening with assurance,
connecting us as brothers, barely flickered
through Thai stick smoke and a Dexedrine haze.
Reeking of white phosphorus and cordite,
you swore that only housecats killed for pleasure.

3 - "Getting Short"

Monsoons came each day those last weeks
just to wash the blood away.
When our mortars hit the marketplace,
the barber's child died. Some stains
don't wash, like the memory of a sobbing man
whose only crime was cutting hair.

That's when I knew you were going home early.
The child's charred flesh made you unholy,
and the shortest distance from Vietnam to Detroit
was through blood atonement—your life for our sins.
When the shot popped, like a pricked balloon,
I realized you had fired it.

But I screamed *SNIPER* to the corpsman,
so your parents could be telegrammed: HERO…stop.
Prying the rifle from your suicidal fingers, I thought,
you should have squeezed the trigger, not jerked it.

A clean headshot, instead of my right palm,
could have closed your eyes.

4 - Aftermath

We both flew home as casualties,
you in your coffin, me in my guilt.
You still deny my absolution
because you took the easy way back, Rick.
The dirt that covers your body now
fills my mind.
Each time I reach for some liturgy
to chant, some Eucharist to swallow
to understand your sacrifice, to bring sanity
inside the empty sound of a spring rain, I choke.

Here, in my kitchen, drinking cheap whiskey
like my mom sent us years ago in shoe boxes,
I grasp for some boundaries.
If only I could leave you there in Washington, D.C.
on a black stone scarred with carved letters
and the tears of your children, unborn and unnamed.

Who's Got the Rada Loa*

I sold my five-dollar Timex for ten to a Marine Corps private named Henry Neville. He said his mamma was a mambo priestess and cast a spell shielding him from the demonic rain of shrapnel that would soon kill the best of us. All he had to do was wear it upside down on his right wrist and wind it every midnight. We slipped off base at sunset to run the clubs and bars on Okinawa, our last chance at whores and laughter before Quang Tri. Henry strutted through the neon streets with square shouldered immortality. His head swayed gently to the rhythm of mamma's three baptized drums and her snake-boned rattle ten thousand miles away, while the copper sound of constant fear dinged inside my ears. Looking for my own protective spirits, I spent his ten on sloe gin and a hooker named Noriko, whose tongue traced the alcohol down my throat and around my navel, heating my blood from the outside in, as if love were an external warmth like mamma's Rada Loa. In the hour that passed, as near as I could tell without my Timex, all of me that was me and all of him that was him flowed from us, pulled by the different vortex of the same spell. I paid Noriko and went to war. Henry, drunk and mugged for the watch, stumbled from the Happy Hotel bar into a back alley, where he bled to death.

*The Rada Loa are the protective guardian powers first saluted in the Voodoo ceremony.

At The Museum of Modern Art

In New York City I Wondered:

Suppose Van Gogh shot himself
in the foot with a rifle, rather than sliced
his ear with a carving knife? Would he be
an artist, or just my friend Williams,
who listed left and limped?

Williams doesn't know Van Gogh, unless
that was the name of the drug dealer
we found on a back street in Saigon.
Maybe there's no difference between them.
Both had beards, red hair, and strange visions
of a world gone mad. Their visions of blue
and red swirled in paranoid pools of color.

Williams drew graffiti on the concrete walls
in Hue, sold his watch for a blow job in Phu Bai,
laughed as nuoc mam ran over his chin
like BBQ sauce, sobbed when the uppers
were gone, placed the barrel of an M-16
against his own foot and squeezed carefully,
as if the trigger would bruise his finger.

After the medics carried him away,
I saw Williams one last time at Leavenworth,
where the Army sends self-inflicting cowards.
I visited on a Sunday. He never spoke,
but like this self-portrait of Van Gogh,
stared wildly over my head, as though afraid
of closing his dazed and moist eyes.

The Pursuit of Knowledge

It begins by counting ceiling tiles during a lecture on fossils.

Seymouria is a reptilomorph named for a town in Texas.
Winged lizards nested on the ground, unlike bats.
Straight-ankle thecodants evolved into crocodiles and humans.

I'm learning these facts because I want to become a civilized man.
In fact, I knew a thecodant in Okinawa with perfect ankles.
Her neck smelled like jasmine and vanilla. For an extra dollar,
she whispered the name of my first love when I climaxed.

I think I chose Karen.

Anapsids, synapsids, and diapsids may have been warm blooded.

The professor's voice flutters along the walls,
a disconnected shadow in fluorescent light
and the girl sitting in the chair next to me is warm,
is no fossil. She smells like honeysuckle,
her hair, the laces of vines in my mind
that must be gently parted to reach a thought.
Her sighs distract me. They sound
like spring rain kissing a small lake.

Vocalization among different groups of dinosaurs
would strongly suggest some kind of social interaction
.

Beside the blackboard, the professor chants his mantra.
I hear the NVA in the streets of Hue
during Tet of '68 before their immolation.
I can still smell the cordite and feel the heat
as we marched the tracer rounds up the pavement
in perfect cadence with the screams.

Some cataclysmic event ended their reign over earth.
All we have left are fragments of their bones.

I'm learning to keep some knowledge from myself,
pretending, as it creeps back into my consciousness,
I'm someone else, an actor in a play
inspired by neither character, nor plot as much
as the numb vacancy in my own voice and my skill at being
what I'm not, perfectly.

On Le La Street in Hue, 1968 & 2005

You were a package that came with this war,
like pound cake & peaches wrapped in C-rations.

The other marines in line by the bunker didn't see your father
place an unlabeled box of condoms on the dirt floor or defiance

shading his black eyes as he yielded your innocence.
When my turn came, I sold my soul for ten dollars,

market price for fresh flesh, and ticked off
"I love you" in a brief stutter.

Now, the words come undone, from wish to nightmare,
become the wet red bandana I placed across your eyes

as propitiatory blindness, a ransom sacrifice of sight
for shame. Now, I've returned to Le La Street, stopped

for white coffee and to stare at the murals on this café wall.
The colors rise in greens, browns, and yellows to reveal

what hides in the beige plaster—butterflies and naked children,
palm trees and elephant grass, rice paddies ringed in bamboo—

each image an optical illusion, like your face I see
mirrored in three young women leaning timidly on the bar.

Each girl hopes that I might wave her over, knows I would
tip well, having learned that in this place of ghosts

my pockets weigh heavy with guilt. On each table sets
a vase of fresh Cac Dang flowers. The floor is spotless,
as though you anticipated my return.

What a Man Really Needs

When I read a list called "What Men Really Need"
last week in some dentist's waiting room magazine,
I remembered you, Rough River Park, and a hawk
bobbing in air currents high above the cave
on the cut bank, untouched by a flushed sun as it
wrestled night for morsels of day, as we struggled
over the hash pipe I bought in DaNang the year before.
Smells of woodsmoke and Mavrodaphne wine
startled me when your hair brushed across my face.
All I could do was scream at the unconcerned hawk,
"Where is your shadow?" "What happened to your dreams?"
I wanted to be alone. I wanted a shot of Jim Beam,
sex without emotion, a line of coke, electro-shock therapy,
sleep without nightmares, a quick death.
Isn't a way to be alive inside himself what a man really needs?
I haven't seen you, Becky, in many years, but I'm still
screaming at that hawk, trying to hang on currents of cold air.

The Art of Deep Breathing

Because I loved blue air caressing the pink canvas
of my lungs I asked the supply sergeant for a gun that worked.
Mine fired one time and jammed. I was green, so he said,
"The Corps issues each jockstrap one gun. Tough luck."
Outside the supply tent, I burned leeches off my left thigh.
The scent of Marlboros sickened me. Thinking of that
fat sergeant, I felt the cold wind as it marched rain
along the Rockpile, down from the DMZ. The scent
of Marlboro smoke sickened me. Thinking of that fat
sergeant's cold beer, and warm tent, I felt the cold rain
fill my foxhole as it marched down from the DMZ.
I hated how he stayed dry while I got wet.

Because I loved letters from Lynn Romer, cookies
mom mailed, photos of sis in her prom dress, perfume
from the envelopes, and a hot shower with real soap,
I asked my Lieutenant to inspect my rifle. He fired a round
at the rifle range. "Works fine. The problem's in your head."
"It won't eject, sir," I whined. "If I try to fire twice, I'm dead."
He refused to listen. "The first man up the hill is a hero."
I thought, the next one is a politician. Armed Forces Radio
Played—*Hey Joe, where you goin' with a gun in your hand—*

Because I loved the swirl of orange flashing behind my eyes,
from adrenaline that embraced the art of deep breathing,
I took my broken rifle on patrol. I dreamed I saw a lieutenant
and a sergeant in my sights. At the right angle, one shot
would do them both. Friendly fire is unavoidable in combat.
No one checks a Marine with a broken rifle. Walking point,

I was an easy target filled with strange thoughts. If only I was in a supply unit as an officer, I would be fat and fearless, breathing deep and firing my rifle at nothing. I never wanted to kill anyone, anyway. I just wanted to know if I could.

Cracked Glass

I once called this man a friend, a beast of burden who
shared my fear of dying, bearing it beside me through

elephant grass, leeches, and brackish paddy water.
We burned those leeches from our backs, walked inside

the scream of Phantom jets and the whine of burning jungle.
In my head Motown music danced, little fireflies of sound

between tracer rounds and the osmosis of earth and sky.
I could have kissed this man a hundred times and wanted to.

I wanted to give myself to the one person who might know
where I was going and wait for me till I got there.

Now, decades later, I'm sitting at my desk
with a cheap, glass-lined thermos of ice and a bottle of vodka,

meaning to share him with the world by breaking lines,
composing words strophes of presence through absence.

Instead, I pour more vodka into the thermos
and crack the glass. You can't mix strong spirits and bitter cold

inside a container made to hold something hot.
I can't remember my friend's name.

Getting Shot

When I recall the first time someone shot me
I think of Robbie with his BB gun, standing
in the apple orchard behind his aunt's house and aiming
at a small spot just left of my sternum. I turned
to run. The copper ball smacked the back of that spot
below my shoulder blade as if a wasp had flown
into my tee shirt and, with cruel intentions, stung me.
Lying on the ground outside the orchard, I asked Robbie
if crying made me a sissy. "Yes," he said and died
two years later in a car wreck before he ever got laid.
Now it's morning, sixty years later. The coffee
in this Roy's Diner is weak. I'm glad. My stomach
sours easily as time slips backward, and I lose my balance
in the haze between where my body sits and my mind dances
with the past. Out the window, I watch the Wabash River slide
through the fog around a bend and cut soil from the west bank,
one grain at a time. The silt disappears by becoming
the current, carried into shallows, swirled over snags, slapped
against the cheeks of stones that line the riverbed until
a sand bar surfaces several hundred yards downstream.
When the first time I got shot became the second, the pain
took the shape of bamboo shoots, rubber trees, and footprints
in the Monsoon mud, but it still smelled like rotted apples
and sounded like the hollow ping of Robbie's laughter.
In the jungle I asked a corpsman if a scream made me a coward.
"No," he said, "just a boy who's a little further down the river."

Absence

I funneled them into single lines
at the roadblock on Highway One,
patted them down for rusty pistols,
fuses and trip wire that made this Tet
deadly for us milk-faced Marines
who stepped off the wrong trail
at the right time; but all they owned
they carried inside them, spitting out
fragments of language in clipped
and broken slang. "Beaucoup mal.
Beaucoup mal. Dien cai dao."

A brown and stunning girl appeared,
held by my hands as if pulled from a hat
or sculpted from clay and light. She shook
only once with fear and the taut spark
of her body jolted my cold circuits.
Then she was gone, running south
with a wave of refugees
toward the corrupt and declining China Sea.

The most stunning girl I ever saw ran away.
She rushed past Buddhist monks, past temples
curling with carved circles and red dragons,
past swirling saffron robes that reflected
the blanched light of dawn and lifted the scent
of nuoc mam mixed with urine and burned earth
like incense. The city of Hue burned on the horizon.

Tonight, as the sweat from a one-time lover
dries indifferently beneath a fan overhead
and I'm bored by the murmur of her sleep,
I drift back to that roadblock and that girl's face,
to her tan cheeks, her thin lips, the slight white scar
beneath her left eyebrow, to her hollow gaze
and boyish breasts. I feel her fingers, frail
yet resolute as a spider's web, wrap around
my wrist, push my whole being away.
I want to taste the red wonder of her tongue, draw
those onyx eyes across ten thousand miles of death
and into me. Instead, I reach for my pants, curse
when my car keys rattle, slip from this motel,
and dream of making love to her
with what's left of love inside me.

Guard Duty in Quang Tri

On those thick, humid dawns
after staring for hours
into a black void, always
I made a cup of instant coffee
by boiling river water
over a blue flame of C-4.
The brown crystals muddied
the clear liquid in the cup,
but a vicious flame reminded me
that I had lived through the dark
onc morc timc.

In Country, 1968

When I read this phrase in a Borges poem –
"the desirable dignity of having died"
I thought of my friend, Rick
sitting alone on that sandbag bunker
ten thousand miles from home his final day
in-country. He must have chosen
the cry of the black kite bird,
the stench of cordite, the sting of blood,
and our last patrol together
beneath the bright blue sky of Hue
over winter in a Kansas full of bad whiskey
and the guilt that grows in the soil of solitude
as the best way to end an exceptional life
when he fired that round through his own brain
and eased his dread of leaving the dead behind.

Snapshots

"I wish I were a camera. I wish it all the time.
My eyes would have a reason, my life would have a rhyme."
- David Crosby -

1 – 1/5/56

How big Aunt Betty's belly
looked when I was eight years old,
how she cried and vomited every morning
for months, even after Doc Peck said,
"There's nothing there but hysteria."
Still, my mother held a cold cloth
to her sister's forehead with one hand,
pretending to feel the baby move with the other.

2 – 1/5/67

Monsoons shot raindrops bigger
than bullets. They strafed my helmet,
a symphony of sameness, a hypnotic
splattered mist that never lifted.
In the bunker I dreamt dry dreams
of Saigon streets - the sway
of rickshaws, rattle of palm trees,
the rustle of silk, the adrenalin
tingling in a French whore,
and defeated the desire to lie face down
in the bright yellow mud, just one more
casualty of a constant dull thud.

3 - 1/5/68

My fireteam eased by a thatch hut, palms sweating,
safeties off, frightened boys on a first dance
with the dying. A widow squatted in the webbed shadows
and picked through a child's matted hair. Her fingers
pulled lice from the scalp. She bit the heads off, one at a time,
while I imagined my body twitching between uneven teeth,
tumbling through betel juice and drool to the dead ground.
That night, alone in my bunker, away from her eyes, I stared
as orange and blue flames from a smudge pot waltzed black
shadows across the sandbags. Even in the uncertain light,
I never lost my focus as a soldier. Even in the soft rustle
of diesel smoke, I never cared why she was a widow.

4 – 1/5/78

Today, four sparrows flew as one bird
from a black bridge railing on the Wabash River.
A fisherman floating beneath me unfolded
his nylon net, feeding the caramel water dreams
of a big catch, while the wind brayed at his back.
He stood in the bow swaying like an unsteady drunk
on an uneven dance floor and waved as if we were
friends. As if we were friends, I waved back.

5 – 1/5/88

My cup left a ring of spilled coffee
on the table. Each time I drank and returned
the cup, the circle became less whole,
rearranged constantly by pressure from a source

it could not recognize. On my plate, two
poached eggs stared upward. I felt the increasing weight
of unbuttered toast in my hand and the slight flutter
of a sparrow's wing in my chest.

6 – 1/5/90

Everything was white, except the blood
and my son's ceramic eyes. How big they looked
for an eight-year-old, like blueberries
in small bowls of milk. Outside the window,
beyond the smell of isopropyl, white snow
strangled the frightened trees. John's surgeon said,
"The tumor's gone, we think. Nothing but air now."
I held a cold cloth to my son's forehead with one hand,
pretending to feel the empty space with the other.

7 – 1/5/2000

From the top of the Farm Bureau Co op
grain elevator, I see the dead tree
in the yielding meadow beyond Lynch Road
where Mike pissed twice on prom night before
lightning split the wood and chased
us along the ground, as if it were a hot yellow stream the sky
pissed back. Mike outran that lightning
till it caught him on a jungle trail outside Phu Bai.
I'm still running.

The Man in the Moon

This morning as I drank my coffee, Henry Tauzin stood
swaying like saw grass in the jungle of my mind. The ebb

and flow of his body spilled over pale light until he became
my man in the moon, a myth born and breathing beneath banyans

as those trees dipped and swirled with the monsoon breeze.
The bamboo played a tango so hypnotic and hollow

I hardly noticed another whistle, the metallic trill
of an RPG ripping through the melody like off key fusion jazz.

Henry heard it coming though. He opened his arms wide,
embraced the blast to keep shrapnel from shattering my skull.

I caught his left arm in my lap, a beautiful Creole arm, tan
and sculpted muscle smoking like a sandalwood joss stick,

gathered the rest of him up and placed him in a body bag
as the moon surrendered promise to the numb shadows of dawn.

Parris Island

The sign reads "We Make Marines Here"

and here is the place
where death began.

Through this gaping maw I walked as boy,
was swallowed, and then disgorged
to foreign lands.
Somewhere beyond
my will to know, I became an old man.

Years past the fear,
swamp,
sweat,
bark,
and bitc of rifle bolt

all suffered for a conceit beyond pain,

I return
without the vicious dream of peace that sustains
a marching army.

I return
to not forget to remember,
nothing kills the loneliness of killing.

Operation Lancaster, 1967

1.

You notice the small things first,
the smell of Sterno-heated C rats, sweat-
rotted jungle boots, and dead water
in the rice paddies. The blanched sun
opens its mouth over the rubber trees
and swallows the last black bite of night.
The metallic trill of a jungle bird
you've never seen hammers morning
into your head like a ten-penny nail.
Phuc Tran's rice wine still burns
through the roof of your mouth.
You haven't even raised
yourself from the hole you slept in
before a dragon fly whizzes by with a sound
like *why*, the single word, that one small word
that brings all these small things into focus
and makes the dawning greater
than the sum of its parts.

2.

Death is buried where you piss and who knows
when the trembling wind will stop.
Maybe, the mist foaming from the mourning earth
or the flesh-colored dust soaking through
your flak jacket will shield your heart and lungs
from the jagged burn of hot metal. Maybe not.

Small beige people glide by on bikes and scooters.
Some wave across the concertina wire
and you wave back as if the wire were not
an ocean, as if you might not have already drowned
them all in your numbed mind. That same sound
whizzes by, louder now than the dragon fly.

3.

So motion is life, you think,
the fuel that fires your green age,
the clack of a rifle bolt
sliding home,
elephant grass churning
like the jade sea at China Beach,
the flutter of your butterfly heart
as it brushes against your ribcage,
the jangle of the wind chimes
on a sentry's watchtower
and the earth spinning so fast on its axis
that you get dizzy when Sergeant Williams
signals the patrol out past an old French
schoolhouse scarred by white phosphorus.

So, motion breeds death, you think,
the force that shoves itself into your throat
from some ancient era of your brain,
the uncontrollable twitch in your left eye,
and the slight palsy of your trigger hand.
You stutter in your step
as you push through the bamboo
to see the whirling point man deconstruct,
spun round, lifted up, pulled apart
by the mine beneath his feet.

You point and fire at shadows
till the shadows shoot back and screams
knead themselves into one long knot
of sound devoid of cause.

4.

You caress your dead like baby birds fallen
from their nests too young to fly.
You bundle them gently into rubber bags
Place dog tags between their toes,
if they still have toes.

But who knows the other dead?
Who cares enough to bury him,
a boy of twelve, asking why
he lies in a pool of brackish mud
stained orange with blood and urine?
Where is his ball glove and Yankees cap?
Who sees his parents shrink over an altar,
lighting sandalwood joss sticks, whispering
mantras that resurrect only smoke?

When you squeezed your trigger and the bullet
punched through the tight jungle air to touch
his chest, did you hope for his death
to be part of something bigger?

You still notice the small things first:
Sweat that stings your eyes while you wait
for the blue cloud of cigarette smoke to ignite
your lungs and a whisper like *why*
as the boy's last breath rushes past his small lips.

The Ballgame

A rain delay, but the field drained well.
Around third base our coach burned
some old rubber tires to dry the puddles.
Black smoke rose as if the diamond
were an altar of burning joss sticks
honoring those among us
who would later be dead.
We lost the game.
We never got our rhythm back.
Maybe we panicked
when the small twister tossed
the grandstand roof across the parking lot,
as if an angry God had thrown it
because it shielded us from the wet wind.
Two college scouts watched me play.
I batted lead-off and "Pumkin" Lambert
threw a slider that ducked in. It snapped
my left thumb, like one of those #2 pencils
Mr. Jones broke during math class mumbling
about his wife and the gym teacher.
My father pulled me aside and said,
"Deal with the pain. The scouts are watching.
Spit and throw a little dirt on it.
That's what men do."
I did and got the scholarship
when the swelling went down.
A year later it disappeared in a flurry
of keg parties, sorority panties,
and enlistment papers.

It kept disappearing when I broke
my mind in Vietnam: unheated C-rations
on night ambush, the whistle of a mortar shell,
a young girl on her back in a bunker,
the stare of her father as he counted the cash,
homemade rice wine and Thai sticks, the giggle
of a stoned lieutenant, napalm at sunrise,
the catharsis of friendly fire
on the landing zone at Khe Sahn,
and the smell of smoking flesh rising
from running children.
Now my *mind* moves
like "Pumkin's" slider. *Semper Fi*
And Dad's advice still saves me.

White Phosphorus

You called him Willie Peter.
He was so close he had to have a name.
Willie became who you were, more than a brother,
a part of blood and bone burrowing those tiny
flecks of fire into a body and leaving
freckle-sized holes for the soul to leak out.

When the shells screamed into the heavy jungle
no one cared about the animals, toucans and tigers,
monkeys and vipers, ducks and water buffalo.
You watched as they flailed and flapped,
pecked and peeled charred meat apart, digging
at the fiery embers one white speck at a time.

You unleashed this monster
with a radio, coordinates, a call sign.
Your fellow Marines laughed out loud
when wounded creatures fled the tree line.
You were too young then to understand action
is character and cruelty is bred as host for fear.

You found four Viet Cong in a meadow
where they died pock-marked, scarred
like lepers twisted and reaching for life
like roots of a Joshua tree. Willie never
asked for thanks. He knew his reward
would come later with another war.

Twilight in a Combat Zone

At dusk time slinks through shadows,
disappears among wendigos, demons, ghosts,
and wraiths that hide in the mist and wait for night.

Minutes dance through your brain disguised as hours.

An unhinged hopscotch of fading light
ends in darkness and orchestrates
a symphony of unseen sounds.

Surrounded by the unnatural splendor
of fear in shadows without substance,
You live like an orchid, the fragile flower
of each breath made more precious and lovely
resting inside the calyx of death.

Meditations on the Jungle Ambush

There were nights, time tied together in thin wires of fear,
when you heard the moon keening as you waited on death.

Its only job was to end your loneliness forever by lighting
a muzzle flash or casting a dim shadow cross a trip wire.

You wanted to believe it receded the tides at China Beach,
captured the leap of Basa fish, reflected a tiger's growl,

recorded the burst of dew cross rice paddies,
and guided the course of a love you would feel one day.

Even the hard click of brass as you chambered a round
seemed romantic in an oblique and ductile glow.

Finally, all it did was burnish, not even from its own fire,
the monstrous clouds roiling above the banyan canopy

and tempt you to forget that each night ambush held
the origin of oblivion in a silent dust of sugared light.

"There is a violent chemistry beneath romantic emotions which is never conducted without collateral damage."

—Sean Norris

When the Stars Go Dark

There are no stars out tonight
in the alley behind Maidlow's liquor store.
Here, Charley Waters used to lean
against another old veteran of WWII
way back in the 60's when I'd come
down the block after high school
civics class and give him my allowance.
"You ain't old enough to drink," he'd say,
buying me a quart of Sterling beer and himself
a fifth of Thunderbird to quench his pain.
They'd sip the wine, he and his buddy,
without saying a word, staring upward,
waiting for stars to pop through
the dusk like white kernels of kettle corn.
I'm in this alley decades later to piss
on the whitewashed wall and look
for those same stars. I've done it before,
bought bourbon and snuck out here
always to wonder, going to my car
as those stars, some ice and some fire,
flowered in the distant darkness,
what Charley found in the vacuum
of the universe that caused
tears to swell in his blank eyes.
I almost had it once when I first came home
numb from Vietnam, a shadow in the mind
forming a vague shape, gathering substance
as it seeped through me like hot tar,
that connection we've all had and lost

with our one beginning.
Tonight, it's possible to imagine again
when all that's above me is a black
well of nothing hung on nothing.
What connects us is our loneliness
tearing through the endless sky,
arms outstretched begging the darkness
for a glimpse of those same stars
that always made Charley Waters cry.

May Fourth, 1970, and 100 miles from Kent State

We are naked
the two of us and sitting
cross-legged on the mattress.

My eyes
into your eyes are blinded
by the emptiest light

I have ever seen. I don't
remember your name, only that here
the warm breath of lavender is crowded
with a distant hint of ammonia
and cordite on the spring breeze.

The song of your breasts on my lips
begins to scream.

Twelve astronauts have agreed already
that the moon reeks like gunpowder.

During death we make love,
an act of survival meaningless
to the ghosts passing over us.

A Vietnam Veteran Visits Hemingway's House in Key West, Florida:

I bought a ticket to your home just to cool off and found it filled with tour guides, scrubbed, sterilized, chanting hollow litanies of ex-wives and the search for one true sentence. Was this my salvation from myself, drifting from one mausoleum to the next, collecting memories like ashes and words like dead flowers? Inside each room your ghost, surrounded by faded French tapestries and photos of dead matadors, spoke of a time when souls were sucked from men in war and only words were left to fill the shell. I felt your presence where you wrote your stories surrounded by cats, staring down the barrel of a fountain pen the way Manolete stared over his muletta, daring a wounded bull one more pass. You counseled me silently, like a Greek god, gun runner, rum smuggler, and master of whores, while I, a teenaged Don Quixote in dungarees, vowed to become your reflection, tilting toward syllables unwritten and searching for ways to exorcise memories. I saw me as you must have seen you, hiding inside the belly of a book from the same rain, mud, napalm, and blood exploding on the same page of a different war. Once, I gathered pieces of a child's father and watched the child cry because the pieces didn't fit. Did you sleep with children's faces in your dreams? How hard was it to live as a legend? How hard was it just to live? Your wars flowed into the waterfalls of famous narrative until language became your life and bled you dry in Idaho. I wanted to reflect your reflection through my own, but an imitation life soon wears like a cheap suit. From the Florida Keys I drove the Pan Am highway, drank Mezcal in Vera Cruz, puked peyote in Guadalajara, screwed whores, ran the bulls, and searched the alleyways and dirty bars of every neon city for the "one true sentence" that would erase the sounds of dying. I never got it right. I never mastered the art of impersonation. The lesson you taught me was one you left unlearned. No man can live forever as someone else, no matter how much he hates himself.

Agent Orange

Fifty years ago, I sat back lit
and entranced by black light beneath
posters of Jimi and Janis. Fried
on speed in a dorm room
paid for by the G.I. Bill, I waited
for the great American poem to filter
through a Dexedrine haze hoping
I could publish my way to fame.

America has always had a chemical formula for success.

Years before I wrote a stanza
I was fogged with tear gas,
dazed by the perfume of naplam
and doused with Agent Orange.

What's a few tabs of Dexedrine to a veteran
who has been swallowed by the wake
of all that hazardous waste?

Sacrifice and hunger
fire and chaos
words.

I believed that nonsense in those
speed-fueled nights pretending
it was real and not a bruise on my soul
that would not heal. Little did I know
that my cells unformed and unnamed

had begun their mutation. Knowledge
would not have saved me anyway.

Words came to the poem
as if I pulled a thread from my war
and the world unraveled—Lapwings
and banyans, bamboo and vipers,
elephants and tigers, a few fig trees
with rhesus monkeys resting on limbs,
the dense beauty of the coffee farms steaming
after a Monsoon rain, the scent of breakfast pho
rising into a diamond white sky and oh my god
the orchids the orchids—disappearing as the planes
dusted the white mist like burning snow across
the jungle where my squad walked a daily patrol,
where mama-sans pregnant with a generation
of dying babies tended the poisoned rice paddies.

Tacitus knew Dioxin as a Roman god
two thousand years before Monsanto
stole his history to strip my jungle bare.

"ubi solitudinem faciunt, pacem appellant"
Where they make a desert, they call it peace.

Passageway

(Vietnam, 2005)

Steam rises from red bricks, the dead
mist of water resurrected.
Incense of fish and rotted wood leaks
from damaged crates loaded
at the Bason shipyard by splintered men.
Sweat claws my shirt and two destroyers glide,
like sharks, to dock beside a bonsai garden.

Un callejon sin salida—a passageway
with no exit—is a Spanish phrase
that might explain my memories,
except I'm not in Spain. I'm on a walkway
beside the Saigon River, slightly south
from Cholon. Moss streaks the water green
and blue as if some numb Impressionist slung
his pallet from one of the small sampans
moored next to a rusted freighter,
skipped it, like a flat stone, around the cut bank.

I stopped walking for a cup of drip coffee
and 555's at a three-sided cigarette stall
where an old man dances with his granddaughter
as Billie Holliday's disembodied voice
"God bless the child who's got her own"
seeps from a turntable through the fog.
Spinning on his remaining leg,
wobbling like a top that decelerates

and gives in but will not quite fall,
he twirls around her, a whirling dervish
with the same urgent need for balance,
the same constant motion, the same
fear of slowing down that makes me feel
faint as I inhale the first blue cloud of smoke.

In a Meadow Where Things Belong

On the small patch of barren dirt
seeded with grass refusing to grow,
a neon green tennis ball sprouts.

I am miles from any tennis court
in a meadow preserved for birds,
squirrels, chipmunks, and worms,

which proves to me that ironic
juxtaposition is a flaw in human
behavior and not the quirk

of a chaotic universe. Reflections
such as this remind me of Rick
our Navy corpsman in combat.

He was a gentle man who cured
sick children with chocolate bars
and patched the wounded as we bled.

One day Rick arrived where he didn't
belong in a meadow reserved for dying
not healing. Not wanting to upset

the balance of nature, he placed a rifle
beneath his own chin and compressed
the trigger softly as if it might break.

Blurbing

A man named Gary wrote a story
about a war we both fought
in different parts of the same jungle.

Instead, it turned out to be about how anticipation kills us.

Once he finished all the writing
and the story got bound in a book,
Gary wanted a famous writer to blurb the back cover.

You know, pen a clever review that points to brilliance within.

Sadly, all Gary got was me.
I liked his story, not in a moral
or tasteful or happy-ending sense,

but rather in an obscene and honest, war is fucked-up sense.

Gary thought my blurb fit sort of well,
like a cheap suit that he might wear
to a wedding or a cousin's funeral,

But he couldn't say how the blurb
made him feel because
he just wanted it to be over.

You might think that Gary meant his story being over.

He didn't.

He was tired.
He couldn't eat.
He couldn't sleep.

The past that crippled Gary was the present.
Waiting for a death that happened decades ago is exhausting.

A Vietnam Veteran Reads the Names of American Soldiers

Killed in the Iraqi War on Veterans' Day, 2005

First, it's about getting through an anonymous list,
Bill Jackson, Robert Johnson Jr., Mike Jones, etc.,
and holding the microphone close enough to your lips
so the clang of barge bells on the river behind you doesn't
drown the syllables drifting like unmoored buoys
through the current of moist air in this river commerce.

The sparse crowd bows a collective head, flags pop, traffic
hisses and slows beside the monument. In the middle of the list
syllables animate my past. Blood pumps through scrawled
letters as if loops and lines were blue veins. Names play baseball,
watch movies, walk hand in hand with teenaged lovers.
I'll never meet any of these men and yet, I know them all

as perfect bodies ripped apart, reappearing for a moment,
before disappearing in the blankness of the turning page.

An Ordinary Man Goes Shopping at Kroger's

(No more to use the sky forever but live
with famine and pain a few short days.)
—Robinson Jeffers from "Hurt Hawks"

Between the basmati rice and the garbanzo beans
an urge for chaos nested in his mind waiting
to hatch a scream. What drove this need
that would embarrass him and frighten shoppers?
Was it the woman who dropped the ketchup bottle
and left the floor bleeding or his own image
in the angled mirrors above the shelves?
Reflection is the mirror's way of dreaming.
Once he dreamed a white tiger in Vietnam, a sign
his whole patrol claimed was only fog until it roared.

From the seafood aisle the stench of fish forced him
to the produce section. Even there, the sweet scent
of overripe Kiwis and organic oranges felt tragic
in a feral wake of swarming fruit flies and housewives.
He valued all that he believed, and thought he believed
all that he could grasp. When does the habit
of pretending faith become the habit of faith?

Intoxicated trees
list roughly
as they drink the wind

He had a student who wrote haikus and joined the army.
Her favorite poem they read in class was "Hurt Hawks,"
she confessed in an email from Iraq on the same day
shrapnel severed her spinal cord. The likeness of her smile
among a group of teens hoping to buy a case of beer
paralyzed his quest for sound. Hushed by memory,
he filled his cart with cottage cheese and frozen dinners.

What is left over
gets carried
in math and in life

A stirring in the ancient sea, where he had come from
nothing and all, where the currents connected him to life
before and after time, gave him the urge to scream.
The line from a poem took it away.

March Is the Cruelest Month

Two Robins and two Jays trill
in counterpoint harmony as if Davis,
Coltrane, and Parker flitted limb to limb.
The birds spoke of drugs and women
through the language of wind.

One leaf appears on a tree
through the bedroom window
and, like a gravedigger might,
you sell yourself the illusion of rebirth
so, you won't go crazy counting graves.

A woman is here and there are the stars,
full of cold fire, lighting your mind
with memory and possibility.
The hooker on Tu Do Street
fifty years ago, wearing a silk *ao dai*

open to expose a thigh
the color of Tupelo honey, reflected
these same stars from different worlds.
You wonder briefly if that might be big
in a Jungian way. This woman lying so near

to your beating heart, a muscle you
would tear from your chest and offer
as a mere token of what you feel,
like a ruby lifted from a velvet box,
reminds you of how the past never

escapes the present, instead of vice versa.
It's always the subtle things—sandalwood
incense, the hiss of the teakettle on the stove,
the flicker of shadows along the candle-lit walls,
that flash the rocket round through your memory.

The room on Tu Do becomes dust
from the cordite that takes away your breath.
The woman who no longer is bleeds into the one
you lay beside. You bury your face in her hair
to hide in the perfume of lavender and fear.

How I Left King Arthur in Vietnam

I buried him with his sword
forged in iron from a burned-out star
in a twisted maze of bamboo and banyan trees

pardoned by death, the madness
in his mercurial blood cleansed
by rocket fire and rifle rounds.

I barely remember him from childhood
when my kingdom was a shrub infested field
nourished by bugs and broken bottles.
With my lance, forged from a hickory stick
and sharp in my dreams, I braved
the perils of attacking squirrels,
butterflies, the neighbor's feral cat,
and with his knights conquered my backyard.

The King and I sprained our wrists, our first wound,
by slipping on a damp patch of early spring grass
into a creek and there, his holy sword began to rust
dulled more and more by disappearing youth,
When he died, I buried him in a place called Quang Tri,

our smiles shattered by memory
if a car backfires, a jet flies low overhead,
the scent of diesel fuel fills the air, or when clouds
form before a heavy rainstorm.

Eli's Elegy

I don't waltz or tango
fly the fly or jerk the jerk
shimmy
bop
twist
or cha-cha
when the jukebox
flays the air with music
in some bayou dive, when
something inside
wants to dance its way out.

But Eli did
with a wide grin all the years
we spent drinking gin, his gold
tooth refracting the dim bar light
hoping to catch a bar maid's eye
or perhaps the promise of a kiss
to ease the sadness of last call.

I don't cry
even though his memories
have killed him finally.
We all die from the guilt of living.
He made his choice
and was made by it when we
came home from 'Nam.
Eli shot his wife through the head
as she lay in bed with her lover.

I will cry once, though,
and I will dance next time
I hear his favorite
Song, *Bon Ton Roulet,* in some
Cajun juke joint near the bayou
that he loved—wild fiddles
squealing in the blue moon night,
zydeco's howling a last spasm
of laughter at my twirling
drunken shadow—Yes,
I will dance, stumble, and cry
into a new dawn knowing no man
can be the man he believed he *was*.

All those years
in prison the rage seeped
from his heart and his parole
became a weight of shame,
impossible to carry with the truth
that the dead are never really dead
except to themselves.

On the Streets of Saigon in the 21st Century

After Reading a U.S. Court Decision
Finding the Makers of Agent Orange
Not Responsible For Birth Defects
in Vietnamese Children:

They swarmed me, like hummingbirds,
a flock of boys two generations from war
twitching so fast in the white sun I hardly saw
the hunger hiding in their dark eyes.
With watches and postcards held aloft,
some scuttled on skateboards while others
scraped kneepads and bike gloves
along Dong Khoi Street dragging knapsacks
full of salvaged treasure, Zippos, rings,
bullet jacket brass, photos, and private things
torn from battle dead many years before
these casualties were ever born.
Their humid voices echoed over traffic
and Claxton's from cargo ships, some moored,
others dry-docked in the Bason shipyard.
I bought a pack of 555's from tiny twins,
maybe twelve years old, maybe fifty.
The acrid smoke veiled the stench of dead
fish rising from the Saigon River as the whole
group hailed a Cyclo driver for my ride to peace,
my reason for return, a ceremony by the Ministry
of Arts and Literature, an invitation to remember,
a celebration of repentance and forgiveness.
Each child waved goodbye as if we were cousins,

ordinary people with ordinary lives.
Some used their only hand, those without arms
shook their feet, three wriggled fingers attached
to legs, one whose torso was backward turned
away and gave me a hug. The twins, fused
at the ears, smiled a bizarre double grin
born from three chipped and blackened teeth.

Transubstantiation

My ball cap faded years ago from indigo
to cobalt and finally, baby blue. Sized the same,
sculpted by sweaty hands, it fits as well as always.

To a Catholic, substance is what it is within itself.
My cap, a gift from Father Bernie, is not my cap
because it is my cap. A little drunk, I think

of Father Bernie who taught me drinking
wine and eating bread at just the right time
is to swallow the body of Jesus Christ

and not be a cannibal. The thought seems
brilliant in these hours of limbo before night ends
and day arrives. I will eat my cap and swallow

more bourbon until this midnight Eucharist becomes
Rick Sweedeen and Dickie Wolfe, Charlie Schulteis
and Joe Sayyah, Jimmy Hayes, and the nameless boy

I shot as in Vietnam forty years before
this night was born. From life to death and back to life,
guilt transformed and the past denied by pretense,

this is the mystery my priest shared as he blessed me
into battle for a country I no longer recognize and a god
I never knew. Substance is what something is and is not.

There's a Lesson for Us on the Perfume River

Litchi leaves, mangosteens, orchids, and flame trees
carried on an August breeze are offered to the river,
whose name is the fragrance rising from it in early fog.
The woman's movements sing a song ancient and ageless
as her parchment face in honor of the river's name.
Beneath the woven bamboo blanket, she lights a fire,
boils her breakfast tea, and then loads a small boat
with baskets of colza, cabbage, fennel, and peppers
grown in fertile soil that bonds her soul to those
who came before and those who will come after.
Her frame, twisted by work and time, begins to pole
through shallows. Her bare feet keep a drumbeat
stern to bow and bow to stern for the melody
of black kite birds, and other shrill harmonies alive
in jungle banyan trees. With the current, she takes
this trip to market daily while children harvest rice
along the riverbank. The sun spreads across Hue,
the Purple City. Her bare feet keep a drumbeat
bow to stern and stern to bow as men pull their nets
of Basa fish to shore through the four Chinese eras,
the defeat of Kublai Khan, the slavery of the French,
and the slaughter of her children by the Di bo Chet.
Not once in two millennium does she ask her god
about the horror of being and the horror of going on.

In the Butterfly Room at the Chattanooga Zoo

(for Brittney)

A Monarch settles

on the wrist of a soldier

deploying soon

to war.

His wife snaps a photo of the bond

and does not know

this instant

will be the one that lasts forever

even if he comes home.

The War Remnants Museum in Ho Chi Minh City

Fenced in by tanks and defused fuel air bombs,
I snap photos of other tourists as they hesitate
and run their timid hands over tools of death.
"Why do we hold sacred the refuse of war?"
My son asks with innocent curiosity as we
stand before the barrel of a rusted Howitzer
beneath the yellowed palms in Saigon.
It has to do with hope, I tell him, not a violent
awful faith in one god's power over another's
or the belief lottery tickets will cure the disease
driving their purchase, not even the expectation
of immortality, but that history may one day
teach some future, kinder people peace.

Peace

A small green fruit grows
only from the earth in Hue. Seeded
by the Trai Va tree, it rises round
and moist in soil blood-red with memories.

I share it now with my friend
Vo Que at the Garden Café
just off a dirt trail in this city
my heart stopped singing
so many years ago, silenced
in a battle to claim what was never mine.

Que and I are two poets who have grown old
by sharing one dream from different worlds.

Here, in this jungle there is a heat of lavender
blossoms and banyan trees that once shaded
tanks, rifles, mines, and death,
we speak of life. A voice within
us both chants in counterpoint harmony
beyond our separate tongues. Sometimes,
it makes the rustle of a spring rain,
the cry of geese in the gray dawn,
the whistle of wet wind through bamboo,
the drum of the Perfume River
beating ceaselessly on the stones of shore.
Sometimes, it whispers like a child's smile
or sunrise cracking a robin's egg sky.

I traveled ten thousand miles and decades
through tormented time and shattered space
to hear this voice rise within me once more,
to share a simple meal with my friend,
who, like the Trai Va, no longer bears me
malice for crimes committed in my youth.

Survivor's Guilt

The dog trots with purpose this morning.
She pulls me somewhere precise and unimportant.
The street swells with silence as I exorcise
a feeling, which isn't real really, more exhaustion
from nightly dreams and the struggle with daily ones,
my regimen for healthy living. I'm okay, the doctors say.
In fact, I'm pretty good in spite of the years spent
wrecking this machine of blood and muscle. If I could
quit this obsession for me by me, I might even be
happy instead of nauseous when my heart skips a beat,
resigned instead of trembling when I remember
one day I'll die and not remember. With the shame
and joy that I came home from war alive, a knowing
grew for forty years, like a stone in my stomach,
all that I owe must be paid one day.
My life will end, not as it should have in youth
quickly when it would have been easiest, weightless
with fantasy instead of heavy with truth.
I'm beginning to understand why my dog hurries
on these cold strolls across the park and into
the woods where I unsnap her leash each day
so she can run free at the same huge oak tree
chasing a squirrel as far as gravity allows, and why
she returns happy that the beast is never caught.

Drilling for Jesus

The dentist spoke of Jesus as she drilled a hole
in one of my molars, how she was reading Genesis
and how difficult it was to follow the Bible from all
that Sodom and Gomorrah sex and blood to Jesus
walking on water or raising the dead because he loved us.
Numbed and nervous, I squirmed through the sound
of torture—the high-speed whir, the suck and gurgle
of a water hose, the agonizing tremolo of smooth jazz
on Sirius radio—and the stench of pain in isopropyl air.
Feeling a twinge of despair and the desire to appear
brave, I shared my pretend knowledge of theology
using a thought delivered to me a priori because I
had suffered neither recent sex nor death, forgetting
in my epiphany that my mouth was stuffed with cotton.
"Hezeus uss who he ussent." "What?" she said,
and the conversation left us both with an existential dread
as the truth misunderstood often will. Jesus was who
he wasn't. We learn when young to hear the lie for truth
if it serves us better. Forget Jesus for a minute.
Think Santa Claus and how easy it was for mom
to get your compliance in the month of December.
Forget Santa Claus, Tooth Fairy, Easter Bunny, think
of my friend Bill who quit school and joined the Marines.
He was a child, neither good nor bad, full of self-doubt
and a sense of duty. Like many of us in those days
that followed the days when our fathers had saved
the world, he wanted to prove worthy of their deeds.
Posters that hung on the walls in the courthouse read
—The Marines Are Looking for a Few Good Men—

and if you remember the Vietnam War, I think you can guess where this is going. Billy stumbled on a land mine with his left foot probably. No one knows for sure because it was one of his pieces we never found. Getting back to Jesus and the hole in my tooth, I said "This isn't the first time things got filled and fell apart."

Lunch at Tri Dove Cafe During the Balkan Wars

You have traveled a coastal road to Piran
and found yourself hungry like the sea gulls
pouting around a barren Adriatic surf.
Old men mend nets on the bows of boats,
a rainbow of canvas sails ripples above them.
The harbor hums a lullaby in the warm breeze.

One bow-tied waiter serves squid with Lasko beer,
the scent of salt air churns beside the sea wall.
Over the sidewalk a boy skates, his legs lift
and fall piston-like in time to metal wheels
along the pavement and clatter of trailing children.
He is a pied piper of laughter and tourist chatter.

Hucksters sell souvenirs from three-sided booths
lined along the quay. Look across the bay.
You can see Croatia through the crystalline curtain
of sunlight that shimmers above the dead sea water.
Smoke from burned towns leaks into white clouds.
The thump of mortar shells and the rattle of rifle fire

remind the dead there why being dead is hard work.
They must convince the living at a safe and quiet lunch
to bear the weight of grief with the taste of tiramisu.

Manifest Destiny

In platoon formation every morning
Lee Jara marched beside me on the base
at Little Creek with more Marines who
waited out their discharge after months
of war for a cause that, by then, escaped me
and I'm not sure Lee ever knew.

He was a friend, Navaho, reservation-raised,
who granted me absolution for being white.
I didn't understand his kindness then, or what
it had to do with irony. Young men like me
born into the color of privilege sing the song
of history with our own melody.

We had invaded Vietnam and dispatched
its people with the same righteous indignation
my ancestors displayed destroying Lee's.
Destiny gets manifested through murder.
I'm seventy now and I have no hope
that Lee's still alive. There are very few

old braves on reservations anymore. At least
he is not here to witness failure. Maybe
they buried his Silver Star and Purple Hearts
beside the bones of his brothers, slaughtered
and sacrificed in shallow graves to make the U.S.
what it never was, to Make America Great Again.

A Peace Group Sends a Veteran

Postcards Noting the Cost of War
in Concrete Numbers Twice a Year

It's necessary admitting the innocent
millions turned into corpses at random
and the trillions of dollars wasted on death.
We seem to have lost track of those figures
in these days of corporate cable news
concerned with recapping and then ignoring
unpleasant holes in life, like a dentist
fills cavities so we can keep eating candy.
But numbers don't always give birth to regret.
The true cost of war is measured
in first-hand knowledge of blood and fire,
by the memory of rape, by an empty
shirt sleeve, by a roiling madness roaring
through sleepless nights, by waves of orphans,
by an unformed sense of dread that freezes time
in some past jungle or foreign desert, by hate
misdirected and anger misapplied to wives
and children, by its unrepentant persistence
in the wounded minds of those left alive.
You can count the dead faithfully and honor
them on the same day every year, lay wreaths
and march in parades that never end.
You can comfort widows and shoot off
fireworks, but you can't measure
relative and connotative words—loss
honor, fear, trauma, stress— or even
peace on a balance sheet in a ledger book
or with numbers on postcards.

Getting a Haircut

1. Hometown

Outside the window
against a gray shroud of sky
starlings by the hundreds roost
like letters in a braille alphabet
on the high wires.

The barber laments firing
his latest assistant as shears
run a ruin around
my nearly naked ears.
In his boredom he will never know

the singular joy added to my trim
by the familiar hum and the scent
of bay rum, by the warmth of a towel
across my neck and tedium that shields
me from chaos for a moment.

2. On the Road

Four dead deer adorn the walls
of Johnny's Barbershop surrounded
by a school of stuffed fish,
a calendar for the auto parts store
that features a bikinied babe
photo'd with a set of sparkplugs,

two bottles of talc, a jar of combs,
and the trill of an overworked
air conditioner. The tepid air hangs
low with a scent of tonsured men
laughing as the bad jokes swim
upstream against subject matter
between Mohammed, slavery,
and the width of a vagina.

One man used to cut
his own hair but says he lost
interest in abstract sculpture.

You wanted a haircut
on your drive to New Orleans,
but you wonder why it had to be done
in Georgia, a place with an uneasy twitch
like the skin on the neck of a horse
when touched by the legs of a fly.

3. Parris Island, 1967

On the cool tile floor
hair piles high like haystacks
burned autumnal from yellow
into red, brown, and black
by a late summer sun.
We wait in a long line
out the screen door. We,
the young who are alive
and some who soon are not,
who began as one of many

sheared bald by the wild rattle
of metal clippers held to even
strokes by machine-like men
until we, the young, become
many of one.

Sonnet in Ben Thans Marketplace – Saigon, 2005

In the middle of morning glories and raw fish, an old soldier
with one plastic arm and air where another should be offers me
a package of postcards. If I buy them, he says he can help feed
his children today and I can show my friends I visited Vietnam.
I tell him I was here in '68 before the truce, when he and I
were young men, when the grass grew high, watered with blood,

when our minds and bodies were whole, when we thought
there would always be enough rain for rice and wars served
a greater good, before we learned droughts, like bullets, come
and go without warning. He lays the postcard in my palm.
Metal joints click like real knuckles, snap and pop,
release their load. But steel is cold and the curtain of pain drawn
across his black eyes tells me nothing of what this man feels
feels about losing the chance to ever hold his wife or child.

A Soldier Returns After the War

Nothing seems familiar here, as if I have gone too far
or not far enough. The ragtag apocalyptic howl
of a radio preacher becomes the hot empty wind
rushing through the pickup truck's open windows as I search
for landmarks on the same stretch of less urgent road I drove
two years ago to senior prom. The gas station has changed
color, the plumber hung new signs. The Smith's soybean field
lies fallow and their children play outside without watching
where they step, without fear of helicopters overhead.
The sky seems blue, but that's illusion. My eyes filter light
to form nature's colors as my mind transfers memories
to my senses—smells of burning oil poured on flesh, screams
of cluster bombs falling, and cloistered voices moaning,
the copper-jacketed taste of hot wind, the clammy touch of night
in a nameless shadow I feel beside me. This is now my refuge
from numbness, the dreadful bliss of arrival home.

Epilogue:

White Noise

I want the same cage that holds
a mime, a cell where bars are made of air
and the door opens like a pair of smooth legs.
Just once, I want Miss America to suck world
peace from a contest judge's cock, a cure
for both cancer and that infection of the mind
that keeps us small. Maybe a cigarette without guilt.

Yesterday, the river reached flood stage.
Brown banks disappeared beneath
brown water. Whitecaps ran, like feral children,
over sandbagged levees.
The hissing, churning, ripping, sucking undertow
sounds like all my thoughts today, like how true
horrors of war both repel and attract. My friend
Marty found this out when he shot
an old Ba in Quang Tri while she slept
covered by grandkids and the scent of ginger
just to see what killing felt like. Then,
put the rifle under his own chin and slammed
a bullet through his cerebellum so he
could find her in some afterlife to apologize.
I loved that man for his refusal to suffer.
Once, no one, not even women, connected sex
to making babies, or understood the difference
between cream pie and chocolate cake
lay more in texture than taste. But, today

I know trees live longer than humans,
that somewhere across town an old Jew davens,
waiting for her husband's ghost to explain
what the dead own.

www.ingramcontent.com/pod-product-compliance
Ingram Content Group UK Ltd.
Pitfield, Milton Keynes, MK11 3LW, UK
UKHW041314190726
13845UKWH00025B/267

9 789363 543829